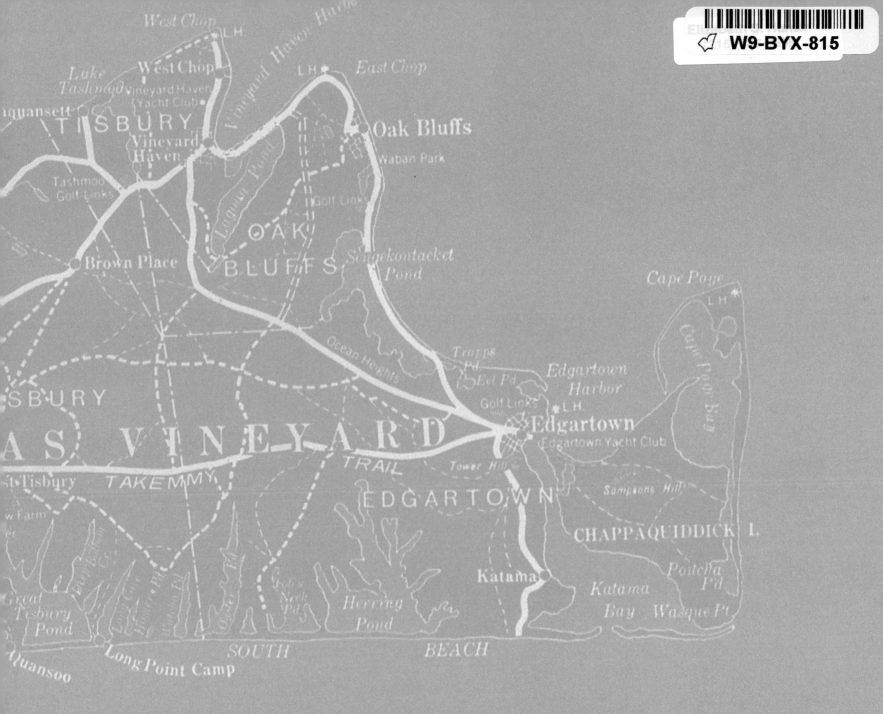

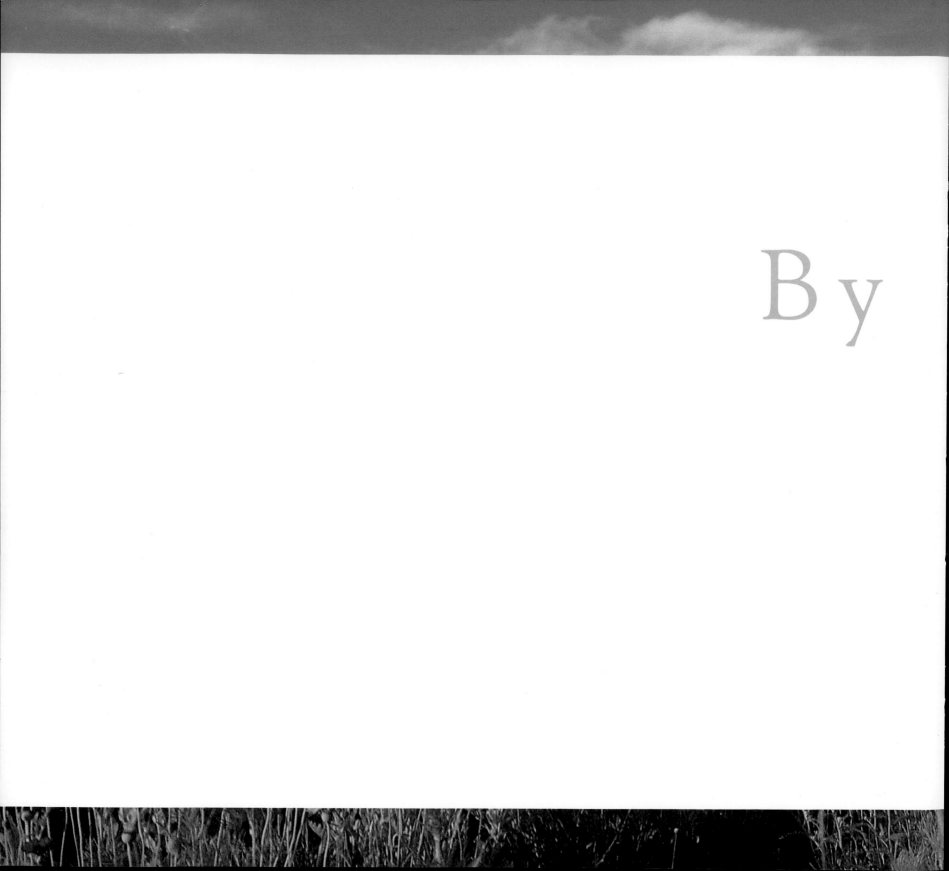

By

Vineyard Light

poems by ROSE STYRON

photographs by CRAIG DRIPPS

introductions by GEORGE PLIMPTON
and PETER SACKS

RIZZOLI
NEW YORK

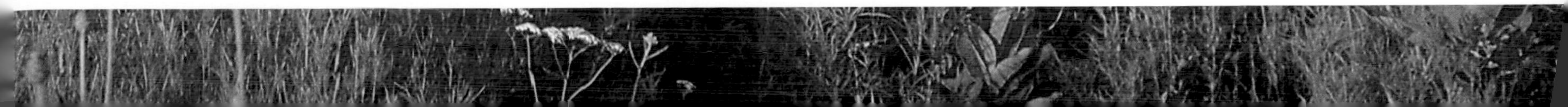

For our youngest, Alexandra,
and for my mother, Selma, and the kin between:
lovers of the Vineyard, all.

—R.S.

To the memory of Virginia Kranz Crossland.

—C.D.

First published in the United States of America in 1995 by
Rizzoli International Publications, Inc.
300 Park Avenue South, New York, New York 10010

Library of Congress Cataloging-in-Publication Data

Styron, Rose.
    By vineyard light : poems and photographs of Martha's
Vineyard / poems by Rose Styron ; photographs by Craig
Dripps ; foreword by George Plimpton ; introduction by
Peter Sacks.
        p.   cm.
    ISBN 0-8478-1871-3
    1. Martha's Vineyard (Mass.)--Poetry. 2. Martha's
Vineyard (Mass.)--Pictorial works. I. Dripps, Craig. II. Title.
PS3569.T89B9 1995   94-43022
811'.54--dc20   CIP

Designed by Nicky Lindeman and Mirko Ilić

Printed in Singapore

About the Photographs 16

About the Poetry 20

No one's awake 24

Katama 27

Wedding Prelude 28

Painted Screen (for Kib) 34

Goodnight, Great Summer Sky 37

Rain 39

Gale 40

Ocean Park 43

Lil's 44

Shenandoah 47

Each Crisp Autumn 48

Death and a Wilderness of Dreams (for Carly) 50

Trajectories 51

October Harbor 53

Forgotten Graveyard 54

Green Games 57

West Tisbury's Fair 58

Blues 61

Fisherman 62

Good-bye Strict Shores 65

Vineyard Light 67

Island Woods 68

Morning Places 71

A Stranger's Beach 72

At Chilmark Pond 74

Elizabeth Islands 77

Seven Gates 78

Long Point 84

TABLE OF CONTENTS

Zack's 85

Black Point 85

The Cliffs at Windy Gates 88

Sand Music 91

Finding Again 93

The Fog Blows By 94

Beach Walk 99

Middle Road 100

Sunrise on Squibnocket Pond 103

Menemsha 106

Oak Bluffs 108

Illumination Night 111

Whiteness 112

Concert at the Tabernacle 114

Tashmoo Farm 118

Cape Pogue 121

Indian Hill 122

The Sunday Bells 126

Taygeta 129

Ballad of Martha's Vineyard 130

Photograph Captions 135

ABOUT THE PHOTOGRAPHS

Craig Dripps is a teacher by profession—he has taught for more than twenty years at Haverford School, a boys' prep school in Pennsylvania, where he is the chairman of the math department. This has allowed him to spend his summers in Martha's Vineyard, where he has pursued his passions for music composition and photography.

He came to photograph by the usual route: at the age of ten or so he was given a box camera with a viewing lid that flipped up. One afternoon during his high school days, he took a picture of a scenic spot on the island—E. B. Keith's pond, a stretch of crystal edged with great oaks and populated with geese (though now, sadly, its water is murky and overgrown with sedge and marsh grasses). Something about his picture of Keith's pond in its pristine days spurred his interest in photography; since those days, graduating from his box camera to a Canon 35 mm, he has gone on taking pictures with considerable success.

From his earliest days, Dripps's subjects were invariably *things* rather than people. His family noticed, and indeed Craig's father made a point of populating *his* photographs with family and friends—"filling a void" as he put it. In the present volume, as readers will discover, the human presence is only occasionally evident in Craig's pictures: a workman in a boat yard, a couple of skinny kids leaping off a sea-bound boulder, a pair of young girls on an amusement park slide, two fishermen, one simply a reflection of the fisherman in the water, as if at the last the camera eye had turned away from humankind. The *works* of man are evident enough—the sweet symmetry of sailboats lined up on a beach, a dory (could someone be lying down out of sight, taking a snooze on the duckboards?), a lighthouse, a beach shack, a gazebo in a winter landscape, an empty hammock strung between two trees, graveyards, the occasional grazing horse, boats at their moorings, an empty macadam road—it is almost as if the photographer felt that the corporeal presence of humankind would shatter the spell of these places.

the fact is that Craig does most of his camera work when very few people are around. He is up at first light, long before the island population stirs in its beds, and thus for four hours or so "the Vineyard is basically mine," he says. He knows every cranny of the island as if he were its designated surveyor. One of the reasons he is so knowledgeable is that he often tutors math in the summer months, traversing the island to the homes of his young charges like a country doctor making calls—carrying with him a schoolbag of marked papers along with his camera.

A summer or so ago I went to hear Rose Styron read her poems in a small gallery where Craig Dripps's photographs were displayed. The room in which Rose sat at one end was packed with listeners, many of them sitting on the floor. Indeed the place was so crowded that, having arrived late, I kept to the adjacent room and wandered about looking at the photographs. The day was warm, and the wide doors of the barnlike gallery were open to a soft summer breeze. I could hear Rose's voice in the next room and the occasional odd sighlike *umm* sound that listeners make when a poem is done. It was my first summer on the Vineyard. I had been taken to many of the scenic views I was looking at in the photographs—Windy Gates and its cliffs, Black Point, Menemsha and its fishing boats, Squibnocket Pond, the West Chop lighthouse, the West Tisbury Oak—and to see these places in the photographs, illuminated by what Rose was reciting in the other room, was to go through a kind of refresher course on the island.

One of the tests of a great photograph is that it tells you something about a familiar scene that you had not noticed before—not necessarily anything specific, but perhaps a mood, or a feeling. How fortuitous that Craig Dripps's photographs and Rose Styron's poetry—to which the same test can be successfully applied—have been combined in this volume: a perfect marriage of word and image.

George Plimpton

ABOUT THE POETRY

Among its other attributes, art may be one of the oldest yet most renewable means by which we can attach ourselves to a place, and thereby to the world. In the poems of Rose Styron, as in the photographs of Craig Dripps, the place is the island of Martha's Vineyard—lit, framed, and focused by the resources of poetry itself. With a versatile grace that shifts between disarming snapshots and longer exposures, her poems bring the reader within touching distance of an "antique landscape / rubbed by hand," and within musing distance of our "mysterious connection with the night, the deep, the shore."

"You come too," Robert Frost wrote in one of his early pastoral poems. Styron's invitation is implicit in her directly shared responses to islandscapes that are at once familiar yet freshly seen: the coves, the meadows, the light-filled bays and beaches, the stone walls and wildflowers, the drifting mist or shine, the sometimes eerie calm that edges toward menace as a storm comes in or a season turns away. Such scenes are offered deftly and lucidly, in words that may startle us to a new alertness, provide us with a verbal island of meditation, or shape an impression that would otherwise have eluded our senses or slipped from memory. So too, here are poems that reawaken an innocence and openness to charm that we might otherwise have lost forever. A deliberately naive rhyme, a lilt and cadence, a fanciful play of associations (stars and minnows, South Beach and shimmering porcelain), all become means of cherishing the world and the perceiver, the sweet motion of the leaves as well as the continuing desire of whoever finds that motion sweet. To dream, to fear, to regret, to let go, to rejoice, to wish again: as if they were inner regions, such capacities are honored here no less than the physical places of the island that bring them forth or that seem to respond to their calling S.

But there is still more to find among these lines, such as the images of friendship, of family linkages, and of the sense that "no man is an island" any more than the Vineyard, despite its relative seclusion, is cut off from what happens across the waters. For Rose Styron, much of whose life continues to be actively committed to the international cause of human rights, the place-names Tashmoo, Menemsha, Vineyard Haven, may find themselves alongside Belfast, Cartagena, Prague. A moment of rural tranquillity may refine an ethical as much as an aesthetic perspective. The sight of a horse grazing through a stone-piled wall may evoke the image of alterable barriers elsewhere in the world—barriers no less between aspiration and reality, comfort and risk, deprivation and fulfillment.

Like the low stone walls that crisscross the island, or skeins of light across the waters and grasses, more motifs ripple through this collection than can be mapped by a casual tour. For that reason these poems and photographs will reward revisiting as they develop associations between each other as well as between the two mediums. One of the strongest yet most delicate motifs to emerge is that of time and its passages. Whether it is dawn, evening, or midnight, or the seasons like strange ferries in their rhythms of arrival and departure, the poems attune such passages of outer time to the inner seasons of youth and aging, of birthdays, weddings, and memorials, of renewals and backward glances. While knowing "how swiftly the starry minnows / disappear," or how summer laughter may echo into a wintry farewell "for us all / departing," the poet has the gift of making what is fleeting linger as it departs. It is a gift deepened by the poetic equivalent of time-lapse photography, an etching of repeated journeys from spring to fall. Styron's gift, complete with gleanings of spiritual intuition, thus becomes as much one of time as it is of place and its hallowing. And through the medium of her words, like the "silvered hay" of that "antique landscape / rubbed by hand," it is in this harvest of poems, of an island, of parts of a life, that we can receive that gift, keep it with us, carry it away.

Peter Sacks

No one's awake
but us, and a bird.
The day's too beautiful
to speak a word.

This antique landscape   rubbed by hand   shines through the mist   like silvered hay

K
A
T
A
M
A

its hewn rail fence   greyed barn, sweet fields   where dusty birds hide   startled, focus day.

Wedding Prelude

I

At Brookside Farm the oxen graze
tilting their horns as harriers glide
aslant the wind, homeward.
The weathered oxcart unused rests
against the welcoming barn.

II

At Brookside Farm the oxen gaze
not from dark-hollowed sockets
mouths agape at ongoing Guernicas.
No masters hanged from the roadsign cross,
no choirboys hidden in chestnut trees,
leaves of midsummer plunging all
around them. No skies spray ash or
blackened rivers bone-full overflow.

III

At Brookside Farm the oxen gaze
on dappled horses—roan, grays—
munching the feathered hillside.
Their gilded tails swat flies,
remembered stars.

From great verandah chairs
the cats uncurl, lions yawning
in their wicker lairs
as I walk by a greener century—
the tumbled birdhouse,
half-tamed pastures, theirs.

IV

What is perfection
but a sudden gate—low, white
in the long stone wall that
frames an English garden?

Three horses, strolling over now
to watch me enter,
nibble an escaping waterfall of blooms
behind the latticed arbor.
Wild turkeys flap beyond them
up into the heavy branches to observe
whatever ceremony.

V

I hesitate, my sleeve
caught on a thorny gatepost vine
of private history, recent untidy dream.
Could it have been this very gate,
affairs ago, unguarded? Then
tarrying inside, bees charging
the blossoms and the laden grass,
I frantic sought for some stone cleft
behind the arbor, a contained escape
to wilderness, and, looking back
from familiar fields
one dreamless morning, pardon.

Foxglove, ageratum, lupine, somnolent
rose I must have planted in my sleep
border the wall again within, unshadowed.
All May, forgetting to rehearse, I'd lie
rabbit alert in the uncut grass.

Green joys tangled my ears.
Nearby crows still ripped the earth for worms
but not a fatal wing whirred past.
Ready for formality again, the wall
surveyed, I heed annunciation.

VI

Whatever ceremony, it shall begin
at four o'clock, surprising as the sky
that clears, the winds that rise
to honor such occasions. The light at four
has followed me through the seasons,
crashing stone-spread clouds
in quicksilver County Clare, arrowing
the cave I shared with hermit crabs
under the clay-dried cliff at Windy Gates,
pacing St. Lucia's rim,

just as the mourning doves that circled
my youth followed me isle to isle
when the steamship pulled away
from Plato's harbor. I would face
those saints and oracles alone
but for the doves' discreet antiphony.
Or as Orion, night after night
so far and dark I sometimes fear to
breathe, holds out his starry sword-edge,
sign: protection. The light at four
returns to the strict garden and
the runaway fields
where goslings waddle to their newborn
pond and turkeys glimpsed at daybreak
balance like rusty gypsies in the tree.

VII

Punctual as light, framed in the center
doorway of romance—the farmhouse
white-trimmed, shingled gray, high
windows that fit his pilgrim heritage
and the windmill standing by—
Zen godfather, freshly ironed
into his oriental robes,
becomes our minister of afternoon.

An hour ago in khaki shorts,
peeled alpine boots, he sent me
scavenging a plant stand
for the stone wall altar, placed
three unmatched bowls for offerings,
and picked a columbine, a bellflower
for the cruet vase.
Unravelling the woodsy-odored cord
from Mary's drawer, he fashioned
delicate whisks from the attentive
pine branch. All concentration,
having touched so lightly
the young bridegroom on his shoulder
with tanned fingers, he is ready,
haloed as our tallest elm
after the hurricane sheared past,
to guide our celebration.

VIII

Groom, godfather—my dearest son, my friend—
I watch you both on Captain Flanders' path,
dragonflies stitching the organdy air,
mayblooms knotting each thread
of tension and affection between us
into a bridal veil you walk beneath,
the puritan winter melted, the slope
and damp stone wall gathering
light for us at four o'clock, gathering
our kin, all children from our past, into
this wedding.

PAINTED SCREEN

Through Chinese screens

rosewood and the pale silk fabric

we call sky

a pure white heron over the water

doubles our reflection:

the artist is responsible

for God, responsible to man.

for God, responsible to man.

the artist is responsible

doubles our reflection:

a pure white heron over the water

we call sky

rosewood and the pale silk fabric

Through Chinese screens

GOODNIGHT, GREAT SUMMER SKY

Goodnight, great summer sky
world of my childhood and the star-struck sea.

White chaise from that ancestral southern
porch my raft,
white goose-down quilt my ballast,
under Orion on the green-waved lawn
I float, high—
new moon, old craft
tide strong as ever to the sheer horizon.

Over the seawall, on the dock
Andromeda their strict and jeweled guard
as tall Orion—seas and lawns ago—

chose to be mine,
our children sleep: Alexandra, Tom
under their folded goose-wing sails
true friends in dream,
the folly wrangle of their sibling day
outshone by starlight.

Calm island evening, never-ending sea—
our lovers' rages, too, are quiet,
drowned.

Miracle of midsummer, the trust of dark
sails us beyond this harbor.

R A I N

Three days rain
or years

willow in the mist
shadow of pale moons

the pond at night
a foreign constellation

the silhouette of enormous
ferns and hollow trees

fireflies before June
new treble frogs

in the close alley
under my skin's feet

white lilac blooming
I never knew before

wet pine needles
pebbles

at the far end of stillness
the dam's steady rain

the first call of death.

Gale

TOMORROW, WHEN WINTER LUCK'S
FALLEN, SAY
MY GRAVE-FINE FEATHERER,
"TARRED YOUR WAY."

WHEN I HAVE SUNG FROM ME
WILLOW AND WING
FLUNG AND STUNG FROM ME
FIDDLE OF DOVES
SUCH SORROW MAY SHUDDER ME,
WORN, ON HER STRING
TARNISH, TRANQUIL ME
DRY IN HER GLOVES
AND DOWN BE MY
SOUNDER DAY.

NOW, CHARM TO THE COPPERY
AUTUMN-NIGHT GALE
SWUNG HIGH AT THE STAR-WASTING
TIDE-WHITE SAIL
LET ME SHINE WITH MY LOVES!

40

Ocean Park

Empty gazebo in the snow-vast gardens
no indigo concert for a sailor's moon
no prince and jester
    conspiring laughter
the lanterned pageant gone.

Where is Oak Bluffs but on maps of summer?
The bugle tapestry, the fireworks hymn
image and echo
    imprint the cold sky
daring our year begin.

Lil's

January.
Ice on the jetty.
Stones blacker than wet
slates after school.
The scary
waters of winter
have given up their feint,
splintered, are still.

At Lil's
a fire, not her roses as I thought
at first, breaks from the windows,
spreads next door
and soon to every easterly
windowpane on shore
as the new ferry
shanghais us out of the harbor.

A memory of Dash
tall and furious glows
and half-blown footprints fill
paths to the beach, the jetty,
crazy forgotten lobster pot
and frozen gull
and laughter, Lil's

across the water
like a final uncomplicated wish
for us all
departing,
echoes echoes echoes
fragile January.

September, and the Shenandoah

fantasy of brigantines

sails to windward, grandly

down the real horizon points her prow

          and disappears. In Vineyard Haven

          we, bereft on docks and lawns,

          dream a last voyage, watch her go

          taking summer with her, now.

SHENANDOAH

EACH CRISP AUTUMN

Each crisp autumn

there are fewer leaves, more clarity—

light cycles of the haymound

odors of late roses

rivers rushing where we

once meandered

content in the casual chaos of each

season, plotting no espionage

because we did not know

the world as terror then.

Death and a Wilderness of Dreams

Death and a wilderness of dreams
pursue my waking.

I have no poem for you this morning
only surprise at friendship and farewell—
the smoky trajectories of stars
echo such music.

Outside my tender cabin
where the wings from evening's butterfly
shone on the windowed midnight edge
of the sharpest crescent moon

shimmering grass belongs to the robins
a white-tailed deer nibbles the garden
ancient lilies open the lake anew.

All my earthly provinces being spoken for,
also my children, my mind empty by way of fullness
is ready for sunrise as the lightening sky.

Death and a wilderness of dreams
pursue my waking
but I am gone.

Trajectories

Déjà vu: I am undone again
by deadline and farewell. Half-
formed questions for the disappearing
dry on my lips, escape my fingers.
Stars I caught a tune from
that first rising
echo no music. Grandfather dandelion,
the dawn moon fades, stranding
my feathers in a meadowed sky
so I must walk from yesterday's
estates to Vineyard Sound, out
into the waves of my unclaimed dreams.

How long can the adventures of a high-
flown season—renaissance in Budapest,
Belfast on the edge, that shining
fermentation, Cartagena's,
keep me from sinking? Tucked
in my matted pocket, salty, limp,
are all the maps of spring.
August wakens me to winglessness
so far from shore.

I float a while
on memory, the hymns of shorebirds.
I hear the roseate tern versing
the light clouds, sail to Gay Head:

> Most lucent bird, thou roseate tern
> white, black-scarfed, saucy
> feathers preened
> smile at your offspring
> nestled in the sand. And if
> the osprey's safely on his perch
> no strangers near, be Zen-of-mind
> and chance an elegant stroll
> along that strand.

No Zen mind here, but still
I watch a subtler creature
stray toward our harbor. Whimbrel,
willet, curlew, who you are
is less important on the dazzled tide
than purity of tone, the sense
I stretch for as you pass. . . .

OCTOBER HARBOR

A POSSE OF GULLS ON OUR DOCK.
ALREADY OCTOBER PREYS
FAT, MULTIPLE, STRONGBEAKED
WITHOUT THE SUN. NO COLORS ONLY SHADES
PATROL THE CLAWS OF BREAKERS.

WHERE CAN IT LIE, THAT FRAGILE LATE SPRING
MORNING, BUOYS CHIMING ON THE BLUE WIND,
THE BAY A SHIMMER OF BELL GLASS
WE'D FOLLOW TO THE SOUND?

WHERE THE SQUALL ENDS
AGAIN I KNOW
ISLANDS, ORCHARDS, REEFS
WILL DISAPPEAR BENEATH YOUR SAIL'S AURORA.

GULLS, GATHERERS OF THE CLAN
RETURNED, FORGIVEN, SHINING NOW
STAND FAST TO WEB ME
FOOTLOOSE PRISONER HERE.

FORGOTTEN GRAVEYARD

Forgotten graveyard sheared by light
this quiet morning of surprise
shimmers with souls from English poems
that roused us each
in clarion days of childhood.

        Now on West Chop Rise
where we slow-waking walk past night
inhaling summer—a lighthouse rose,
blossoms tumbling by a pasture gate—
before the politics and rhymes
of noon define us

        faces once close tease.
Light through the fence intensifies
and this desire: no midday come,
I in that corner by the ancient stone
shadowed
        again, alone
the world going by all afternoon.

        I do not mean forever.
Given
choices for home or the farther climb
tomorrow some bright road I'd choose,
friendship and walking on.

GREEN GAMES

Heart of the island, this centuried oak
green-crusted octopus bared as we chase
last leaves down the windtunnel streets of November
beats in our winter limbs
strong as the memory of sea.

Inland the children curl slow over strategems,
gravity's cities. Come June may they wake
to imagine-remember swift climbs and green games
in its branches, seize
summer's simplicity.

West
Tisbury's Fair

the ferris wheel is going up
the carousel and little cars
are getting ready for my ride
around the earth and to the stars

puppies and ponies at the fence
fiddles, aromas on the air—
what summer prize might I win tonight
in paradise, West Tisbury's Fair?

BLUES

Fishing for blues
from the afternoon jetty
the man of our dreams
takes a god's silhouette.

By eventide casting
his lifeline arcs, glitters
against this blackness.
The moon's minaret

(a lighthouse at sunset
winged raptors around it
its beam through reluctant
darks circling us home)

has caught him believing
in the power of midnight
our starry souls
scattering the foam.

Fisherman

MILES SOUTH AND OUT OF GAY HEAD
WEST PAST MENEMSHA BIGHT
WASQUE SILVER CHANNELS EAST
RIFFS NORTH AND ICY SOUND

THROUGH TURNER'S RADIANT SEA HAZE
VERMEER'S LATE DELFT BLUE LIGHT
ON CHARCOAL BAY OR BLEACHED LAGOON
OR MERCURY-MIRRORED POND

A LONE BOAT'S CASTING, TROLLING,
RIDING ANCHOR, SILENT, SKILLED—
LUCK'S WARRIOR, ISLAND FISHERMAN
BEHOLDEN NOW TO NONE

THUS HERO TO US MORTALS, THRALLS
TO SKY AND SHORES WE'VE WILLED.
HIS MYSTERY: WORK,
ADVENTURE, LOVE ARE ONE.

Good-bye Strict Shores

Good-bye strict shores!
The sea's upon me.
I am gone
into a wilderness of waves.
The sky showers
incessant minnows.
The mud nourishes
my seaweed shroud.
The water's breath
in my breathless space
blows green as the stems
of Queen Anne's lace,
sweet as the motion
of leaves, desire
that led me early here.

How swiftly the starry minnows
disappear.

VINEYARD LIGHT

To live in a lighthouse,
cloud islands by
the tide lazing in
the steamer's farewell
the tall ship's sail
against sunset fires
as dusk descends
a Thanksgiving sky

awaiting snowfall
as you and I
await desire's
white harvest

to walk the fields
where wildflowers shone
(fog waves its wand:
the trees, the sand
seawall and spectrum
landscapes gone)

when the world invites us
to disappear
the foghorn hollows
a cave of air
and the lighthouse beam
like a soul's high flare
illuminates God
first there, now here

inside: safe midnight
fog at seven
we still unclaimed
by the buoy's clanging
the bustle of town
the arriving ferry

high in our stairclimbed
crystal aerie
the foghorn intoning
heaven
to live in a lighthouse
or just nearby
was childhood's dream.

ISLAND WOODS

Come walk with me
in the West Chop Woods
when the sun has burned the sand,
wild breakers batter
our fishing rocks
or the streets to town are jammed.

Walk barefoot along
its earth-soft trails
overhung with oak and pine.
Let your pup chase squirrels
or surprise a grouse
where the huckleberry bushes shine.

Or come next May
when the fern spreads green
and the lady's slipper first uncurls
and the white pole risen
at the wood's far edge
its American flag unfurls.

Beyond this kingdom
the lighthouse waits
fairways and the tide-ride shore,
but the path disappearing
at the fallen tree here
is one we must explore.

A cardinal's flash,
a monarch's flare,
through sky-frames the arrowed geese—
come walk with me
in the West Chop Woods
on our many trails to peace.

MORNING PLACES

WILD INVITATION
AT THE CLOSED WHITE GATE

TAMED STALLION GRAZING
THROUGH A STONE-PILED WALL

ROSARIES OF BIRD SONG
COUNT THE EARLY LIGHT

AS OLD BARRIERS ALTER
UNDER SUMMER'S BLOOM

IN CHILMARK
IN CAPETOWN, LHASA, PRAGUE, ALL

THE MORNING PLACES
CLAIMED TOO LONG BY DREAM.

A STRANGER'S BEACH

A stranger's beach, trespassed in December
Draws all the skillful edges I shall never
Find upon my own. The early sun
Defines the sea, the rough-shelled sand, clover
And cliff, as an instructor in Man-
As-Mathematics might rig a sum
Or two for me, proving that I could solve
In numbers what in love I'd overdraw, involve.

See how those rocks, toy boulders
Piled against Europe's ocean there, defend his land?
Now before school the young lord may stalk down
Pail-armed, from his father's sleeping shoulder
To forge his road, build his own castle, plan
Armadas. Yet see, in this winter dawn
Where the rocks end, small waves curve the sand
And there, fortressed by toadstools only, the grasses bend.

AT CHILMARK POND

At Chilmark Pond a cove of fog
hallows July this afternoon

pale skiff at rest
my history bears
softly: blurred grasses, disappearing dune.

The shreds of nightstorm,
lasering sun,
torment and first release, noon rain

in this found haven over Abel's Hill
exist not, all horizons gone.

ELIZABETH ISLANDS

THE BLACK ROCKS OF CUTTYHUNK
ARE DIAMOND IN THE SUN

                    THE PALE HILLS OF NAUSHON
                        WITH SHEEP ARE OVERRUN

NONAMESSET, PASQUE
    AND NASHAWENA GLEAM

                        BEYOND MY SAILS IN BLUE JULY,
                            THE ISLANDS OF A DREAM.

            SOME NIGHT IN AUGUST
                WHEN HARBORS ARE ASLEEP

                        I'LL SAIL ACROSS TO NAUSHON
                            AND COUNT THE MAZE OF SHEEP

AND IF, WHEN STARTLED COCKS CROW
THE WIND FOR HOME HAS DIED

                        I'LL DIG THE DEEP BLUE MUSSELS
                            FROM THE MORNING TIDE.

Pitchdark.
The saltworks beach at Seven Gates
looms in my headlights: end of the pitted road.
Guilty of plotting trespass,
the site sacred beyond my noon imaginings
and not believing I would dare arrive,
I flip off my lights, sure the bass
will recognize me and retreat.

Thoreau once sensed, some fish all their lives
and never sense the fish are not the quest.
Nor are they mine, exactly, though tonight
I cannot guess what is: mysterious
connection with the night, the deep, the shore
I've come to uninvited. "Flyrods," my muse
has whispered, "unreel the most direct
lifelines to the soul."

Glass afternoons
I have watched
those islanders I long to understand
cast from the pier or jetty
or skim by in little boats,
stand still, send a costly filament
into the bluebottle air as if to catch
a roseate tern, an osprey gliding home.
The line would make a rainbow, descending as
it did against the sun—holding,
till the sea-patch darkened, spurted upward,
spewing a pewter flash, a luminous child's rocket,
caught, or disappearing downward, pearly grace and gone.

At midnight once I saw three pillared
silhouettes of gods, at sand's edge, working
the tide. The slim moon rose without a star
to guide it. Over the blackness—meadow,
current, sky—only the lifelines
gleaming, caught me, and the firefly
on the wave. Aeons earlier it seemed
I'd cast, myself, from major crafts
on heavy lines, cold mornings. But that
was artifice, and though my wrist still feels

SEVEN GATES

the pull, my throat the rush it felt
facing my quarry—
alarm because I knew
I'd not release it, others watching—
largely I have forgotten.

Now the narrow five-plank pier
stretches into darkness—danger—
lightening a bit as I, breath held, tiptoe out.
The dark will be as daylight
if I stand here long enough, and listen
for the splash, somewhere below. Waiting
as if the meaning beneath a lover's
sadness, his distraction or opacity,
could in the coming moment be revealed.

Silence. Shadows. Something else is missing.
Hope fails my long, slack line.
Is it the fireflies,
come with their offspring one by one
to the black scrub thickets
on the duney hillside now, flashing
tiaras at the sky's rim?
Perhaps they have been absent all these seasons
because I caught so many
artlessly on our childhood lawn,
believing the alchemy of their flame
must mean they loved my catching them,
that they'd found me.
Perhaps they have returned, trusting me
not to close them in a jar.

Who is it that can trust himself
the landscapes of temptation now so changed?

The line bends lightly first, sudden, strong. I pull
gently and then hard the other
player to my dominating hand.
Will I be able to release him from my hook
to mark exactly how that platinum streak
finds farther depths, that he might
find me, afterwards,
north at the sea's spire?

Long Point

A MILE AND A HALF
      ALONG SOUTH BEACH
AS FAR AS MY SUMMER
      EYE CAN REACH
THE SAND IS ICED
      WITH COLORED SHELLS
SHINY AS EASTER
      HUSHED AS BELLS

ARE HUSHED THIS MORNING.
      THE ISLAND SLEEPS,
ALL BUT ONE
      WHO A CALENDAR KEEPS
AND, RISING EARLY,
      BLOWS OUT THE MOON.
SOMEONE IS HUMMING
      A BIRTHDAY TUNE.

Zack's

The lure of South Beach
　　on a beautiful day
the crest of September
snow kingdom's December
blue windward and leeward in May

the lure that the curlew
　　and sanderling know
of wildness and bluster
of limbo and luster
sun chasing the tail of the blow

when life is intense
　　or contentious in town
too calm at the harbor
too rich by the arbor
the lawn in this heat turning brown

the lure like a rainbow
　　He claimed there should be
stormcast to tease us,
catches us, frees us—
Come, Love, let us race to the sea!

Black Point

SOUTH BEACH TODAY

ALL BLUES AND SHIMMERING GRAY

LIKE DANISH PORCELAIN

MAGNETS MY SENSES. I

CHOOSE OPALESCENCE, SHELL

SECRETS ONLY MERMAIDS TELL.

AND WILD WHITE SWANS

ASTONISH THE SKY.

The Cliffs at Windy Gates

High fog: the sky is going,
the cliffs at Windy Gates
hang in an august dawn.

Mysterious as monks minding Tibet
we descend, unseen unseeing
each breath counted
all the way down.

Flatness reassures
our soles, the damp
grained sand.
Boundaries:
precarious clay wall
and petticoat sea.
This great lost beach
trusted once more is ours.

Now, centaurs and their quirk
reflections in the surf
come over the far sands
pounding, pounding.

At the sea's edge
sun-sensed we stand
arms wider for the wind
the clearing sky
to welcome those familiar creatures
man-and-beast, skewed mirrors
gone in the stillness of low tide.

SAND MUSIC

Falling asleep
on the beach in September,
the last ferry's oboe gone,
I am caught in the cobwebs
of dusk in the hammock
of wickets that sprouted
croquet on the lawn,
of lattices climbing
with trumpets and moonseed
and clouds in their haloes
at dawn.

F i n d i n g   A g a i n

FINDING AGAIN THE SECRET TREE-DARK PATH
FROM HEROES AND THE WORLD OF ORDER HIDDEN,
TRACING ITS LEAFY ARCS, THE PUNGENT ARBORS,
THE REDSTART BEAKS NIBBLING AT DAYBREAK'S SILENCE,

CLIMBING THE ROCKY STEPS NOW FAR FROM HARBORS
WE QUICKEN, CAUGHT IN MIDSUMMER TORRENTS
OF OLD ANTICIPATION. THE OPENING — SKY
THROUGH PALE VENETIAN PRISMS DAZZLES THE GRASS

AGAIN, BEYOND THE LAND DAZZLES THE OCEAN.
BUT, FOOTFAULT. THE CLIFF-EDGE — JAGGED SUDDEN
CLEFT BY OUR RECENT WINTERS OF EROSION
THE GOLD MAPPED BEACH DOWN THERE, NO STAIRS, NO PASS

YET CHILDHOOD'S BRINK HERE OFFERED TO MADDEN.

STAY? RETRIEVE THE DARK? TAKE HEROES' MEASURE?
THREE TIDAL KNIGHTS HAIL US AND CANTER BY.
"HURRY," THEY CALL, "LEAP DOWN! WE'RE OFF FOR TREASURE!"
SUCH WILD CHOICE RAVELS MORNING, FORBIDDEN.

THE FOG BLOWS BY

The fog blows by
returns, seeking Squibnocket's dune
obscures the sky
pond grass rocks shoreline and soon
the last of summer
friends climbing the steep chalk sand.

Imagining sunset in the wilderness
as one they stand
till dark.
Then something hovers, beats,
takes wing.
High-balanced, Tess and Rosey part
veil after veil of air

while Constance leaves for love's adventuring,
and Lucy's gone to cut her summer hair.

Beach Walk

I'm older than these spiky cliffs
and older than the sea,
walking the silent sunrise beach
there's no one old as me

no one to think of deaths to come
nor watch our footsteps fading
fast in the sands of morningtide
where the wind and I go wading.

99

MIDDLE ROAD

The double line
from Chilmark winding
leads me where
I cannot say
I love you
down the pitch of road
the steeper tide
this green and empty day.

SUNRISE ON SQUIBNOCKET POND

Sunrise on Squibnocket Pond
September out to sea:
a fleet of pirates—parchment swans—
sail to the edge where summer's gone
in fierce array
hold fall at bay
one morning more for Lucy, me.

Slant rays seek a roseate tern,
brilliant we glide from shore
across the silence swift and clear
as friendship or tomorrow. Near
blue herons dream
the dunes between
parting and here.

MENEMSHA

Scarlet sunset at Menemsha
sailors, fishermen all home
their craft and armor anchored
where we lie
watching a light wind's afterthought
stir the September harbor
masts gently joust
the deepening evening sky.

OAK BLUFFS

IN SUMMER THERE'S A MAGIC TOWN
(THE TOWN WHERE I WAS BORN)
WE VISIT WHEN THE SUN GOES DOWN
A MAGIC, MARVELOUS NIGHTTIME TOWN
WHERE A HUNDRED FACES ARE THE FACE OF A CLOWN
AND A HUNDRED SOUNDS A HORN

A HORN THE PIPER MUST HAVE PLAYED
IN HAMLIN LONG AGO
WHILE MOTHERS WATCHED THEIR CHILDREN FADE
DOWN COBBLED ALLEYS, UNAFRAID—
THESE ARE THEIR KINSMEN, ON PARADE
IN THE MAGIC TOWN I KNOW

WHERE CHINESE LANTERNS LIGHT THE TIDE
TO STREETS WHERE SWEETS ARE SOLD,
BRIGHT MUSIC BLARES AND PINBALLS SLIDE
AND LACE-TRIMMED HOUSES GLOW INSIDE
AND I ON THE FLYING HORSES RIDE
AND CATCH THE RING OF GOLD—

"OAK BLUFFS!" THE WINDS OF AUGUST CRY
"OAK BLUFFS!" THE SEAGULL CALLS.
WHEN DAY AT LAST HAS LEFT THE SKY
AND THE BEACH IS COLD, MY HEART CLIMBS HIGH
AND FOLLOWS THE WIND AND THE SEAGULL'S EYE
AND FAR WITH THE COMET FALLS.

ILLUMINATION NIGHT

The sky is dark
old lanterns glow
beneath the leaves
through cut-out porches
belfry, balconies,
bannister, eaves

The Oak Bluffs moon
captured, parcels
its orient beams
enchants us strolling
one last hour
free as our dreams

WHITENESS

Every April when our plum tree
spreads its wings in wedding bloom
I am again obsessed by whiteness—
whiteness, rhyme, and Rome.
But April's over the hill this year,
and I have promised not to rhyme,
and Rome where love began again so often
is abandoned.

Whiteness remains: obsessions: tall
sails rounding East Chop harbor,
cloud flotillas through my kites,
swans racketing above the dunes,
bleached alligator skeleton and
paper butterfly washed up from the
Okavanga on the long white
breakers that devour my shore.

Or, summer slipped away: a wide
verandah rocking to Virginia,
white pillars holding up the James,
Polly's commencement dress fluttering
in the attic storeroom whose window
will not close this autumn, strands
of a memoried grandmother's
unpinned hair. Even
the ice that held our skateblades up
is disappearing under snow,
knobbed white-stocking birches
our replacement.

Tomorrow, what shall I do
with whiteness? What is there about
mortality, immortality, when great
white birds take wing? Memory walks
a Himalayan ridge, between high
spaces, old friend standing
on the last field-edge behind me
counting disappearing yaks,
old friend striding oblivious ahead
toward Nirvana, each of us balancing his own
present destiny

in Bhutan's white kingdom,
Buddha's tiger waiting
at the monastery, snow falling,
falling, white and unseen cranes
asleep below.

To waste these days! The wind
still shimmering each high bouquet,
—these nights! The Milky Way,
old Pegasus who dives outside my
window, scattering moonlit seeds
white on the farthest wave.
Sheer curtains billow, but I cannot
close the casement on such fantasy.

Concert at the Tabernacle

Laemmergeyer gliding
the high Rift Valley
small plane humming
where Manyara gleams
herds of wildebeest
below us roaming
reel in
our flight of dreams.

Green leaves feather
the Tabernacle
the sun keeps time
as the music flames
angels are tilting
to a blue guitar
this Sunday in September
our enchantment: James.

TASHMOO FARM

MIST CURTAIN RISING AT TASHMOO FARM:

BLACK FENCE, BLACK TREES EMERGE AS GRAY,

BLACK HORSES SWEEP THEIR CHESTNUT TAILS

ACROSS THE WATERED SKY, WELCOMING DAY.

ALERT THE BRIGHT-WINGED HARROWED FIELDS,

GREEN HILLY PASTURES WILDFLOWER-STARRED,

THE BERRY TRAILS, THE SUN-GEMMED LAKE:

DAUGHTERS ON STEEDS, BY NATURE CHARGED

WILL SOON BE FIERCELY TROTTING THROUGH

EACH OF THEIR SUMMER PROVINCES TO GUARD.

CAPE POGUE

When I am old as Socrates
and suns have bleached my mind
with herring gulls I'll sail and dive
this golden Vineyard strand.
Starlight will comb the looking glass
all glittering days behind
as I follow silver minnows
into wonderland.

A Vineyard place
of undeciphered signs. The road stands still,
widens among the flints and copper ferns
and climbs
a grass-abandoned hill.

Oakleaves rustle underfoot, charged,
wary of rain.
November's sun, sly laser, streaks a field
drowsing to Indian glory as if done
with the nourishment of grain.

INDIAN HILL

Savannah sparrows in the empty furrow play
hopscotch, a southern tune.
Red squirrels from my childhood leap the air.
A crow is king in the peeling sycamore.
The clarion loon

turns every wind-belled charm
toward golden dangers:
a fall from limbs of grace, release, be found
as leaves brighter than autumn jewelry floating
the walls sands buoys of Vineyard Sound.

I have been afraid to lose my way, desire
magic of summer, the extending light,
afraid of scholarship's intensity
staring alone
down every traitor height.

Or poised to follow where the snow moon sailed
I'd court its misty brilliance till the true
moon stared back, beckoned. Then I'd deny
the night's wit and the stars'
laughter, the sweet tide. Rue, rue.

Sunset will come, and winter
but through the always anguished-and-too-early
dark I sense they scheme
to haunt no longer all my Chilmark
sanctuaries, only illuminate

those manuscripts, this harvest, buried dream.

The
Sunday Bells

The Sunday bells from island towns
chime down the harbor, up the lanes
where you and I
abed still lie
humming the night's romantic tunes.

White spires that pierce those royal skies
prick not our consciences nor tease
our common hearts
when summer charts
celestial Vineyard days.

VEGETATA

Once, before the sun went down
I saw three gulls at Edgartown

wheeling, wheeling round a mast
empty of sails. As if time past

had come again, as if this harbor
greening wild, bloomed as an arbor

still: no lighthouse, no sure dock
or perfect dwellings, only hillock
and vines tumbling with grape and plum,
and myriad sands—he too had come
this tired sailor, under his mast
stretched out dreaming. His eyes, cast

upward to gauge the gulls' courage
a world ago, before his voyage

was over and lost and won,
are furled with the sun.

BALLAD OF MARTHA'S VINEYARD

My island in the morning
is the palest porcelain sky
a gull call and a whistle
and the ferry gliding by

clematis spilling on the hedge
and children on the pier
and sounds of summer everywhere
I turn again to hear.

My island in the morning
is blue enameled sky
clouds that hide a thousand kites
and sailboats slanting by

grasses to rouse my early feet
shells to rule the sands
and miles of crystal mirroring
the long-bright lands

'til fountains, far Ravello,
ruined temples on the Nile,
old libraries—Isla Negra's—
or Zanzibars beguile

and labyrinth and white fjord
volcano, cave, and cay
and spice routes to the Orient
set spinnakers for me.

Returning with the morning
a pomegranate sky
the bay a pewter symphony
as geese go honking by

and mica panes that glisten
from houses on the beach,
the lighthouse like an Indian scout
measuring autumn's reach,

I sight a Vineyard harbor,
a foil and tissue sky,
the echo of a foghorn,
an airplane silvering by,

a sea of opals breaking,
a moonshell opening wide,
and fishermen gone seeking
where the lucks of winter ride—

O, stay as morning, Island,
a changing song and sky
a lover, a deceiver
while my life goes skimming by

in stormclouds and a racer's wind,
fresh rain and spits of foam,
the bay a sudden topaz
and a rowboat coming home.

PHOTOGRAPH CAPTIONS

page 1: Chilmark Surf

pages 2—3: Lucy Vincent Beach

pages 4—5: Wildflowers, Chilmark

pages 8—9: Lillian Hellman's Beach Shack, Gay Head

pages 10—11: Waiting for Spring, Tashmoo

pages 14—15: East Chop Yacht Club

pages 18—19: On the Waterfront, Vineyard Haven

pages 22—23: October Condiments, Chilmark

page 25: Playing in the Morning Mist, Lucy Vincent Beach

page 26: Antique Landscape, Katama

page 29: Garden Gate, Brookside Farm

pages 32—33: Brookside Farm

page 35: Mill Pond, West Tisbury

page 36: East Chop Lighthouse

page 38: Until Next Summer, Chilmark

pages 40—41: Autumn Gale, East Chop

page 42: Snow-vast Gardens, Ocean Park, Oak Bluffs

pages 44—45: The Docks of January, Harthaven

page 46: Shenandoah

page 49: Fall Harvest, Edgartown

page 50: Patsy's Porch, East Chop

pages 52—53: Sea Gulls on the Posts, Oak Bluffs

page 55: On West Chop Rise

page 56: Centuried Oak, West Tisbury

page 59: The West Tisbury Agricultural Fair

pages 60—61: Fishing for Blues, Vineyard Sound

page 63: Heading Out, Menemsha

pages 64—65: South Beach

page 66: Circular Stairway, East Chop Lighthouse

page 69: Island Woods

page 70: Chilmark Pastures

pages 72—73: Winter Beach, Katama

page 75: Chilmark Pond

page 76: Island Sheep

pages 79—80: The Coming of Night, North Shore

pages 82—83: Vista from Windy Gates

pages 86—87: In Winter's Grasp, Katama

page 89: The Cliffs at Windy Gates

pages 90—91: Off Moshup's Trail, Gay Head

page 92: The Cliffs of Gay Head

page 95: Along South Beach

page 96: Edgartown Lighthouse, Fall

page 97: Edgartown Lighthouse, Winter

pages 98—99: The Cliffs of Lucy Vincent Beach

page 101: Middle Road

page 102: Parchment Swans

pages 104—105: Guitar Pond

page 107: Fond Memories of Lobsterman Donald Poole, Menemsha

page 109: The Flying Horses, Oak Bluffs

page 110: Illumination Night, Oak Bluffs

pages 112—113: Along East Chop Drive

page 115: The Tabernacle, Campgrounds, Oak Bluffs

pages 116—117: Tashmoo Farm

page 119: Barn at Tashmoo Farm

page 120: Herring Gulls, South Beach

page 123: Indian Summer

pages 124—125: Sunday Morning, Edgartown Federated Church

page 127: Carriage House, Charlotte Inn, Edgartown

pages 128—129: Edgartown Harbor

page 131: Morning on East Chop

pages 132—133: Reflections of a Menemsha Fisherman

page 134: Alley's Store, West Tisbury

page 136: Lazy Afternoons, Vineyard Haven